colegio - school 2
viaje - travel 5
transporte - transport 8
ciudad - city 10
paisaje - landscape 14
restaurante - restaurant 17
supermercado - supermarket 20
bebidas - drinks 22
comida - food 23
granja - farm 27
casa - house 31
living - living room 33
cocina - kitchen 35
baño - bathroom 38
cuarto de los chicos - child's room 42
ropa - clothing 44
oficina - office 49
economía - economy 51
ocupaciones - occupations 53
herramientas - tools 56
instrumentos musicales - musical instruments 57
zoológico - zoo 59
deportes - sports 62
actividades - activities 63
familia - family 67
cuerpo - body 68
hospital - hospital 72
emergencia - emergency 76
Tierra - Earth 77
reloj - clock 79
semana - week 80
año - year 81
formas - shapes 83
colores - colours 84
opuestos - opposites 85
números - numbers 88
idiomas - languages 90
quién / qué / cómo - who / what / how 91
dónde - where 92

AF219232

Impressum
Verlag: BABADADA GmbH, Nedderfeld 112 , 22529 Hamburg
Geschäftsführer / Verlagsleitung: Harald Hof
Druck: Books on Demand GmbH, In de Tarpen 42, 22848 Norderstedt

Imprint
Publisher: BABADADA GmbH, Nedderfeld 112 , 22529 Hamburg, Germany
Managing Director / Publishing direction: Harald Hof
Print: Books on Demand GmbH, In de Tarpen 42, 22848 Norderstedt

colegio
school

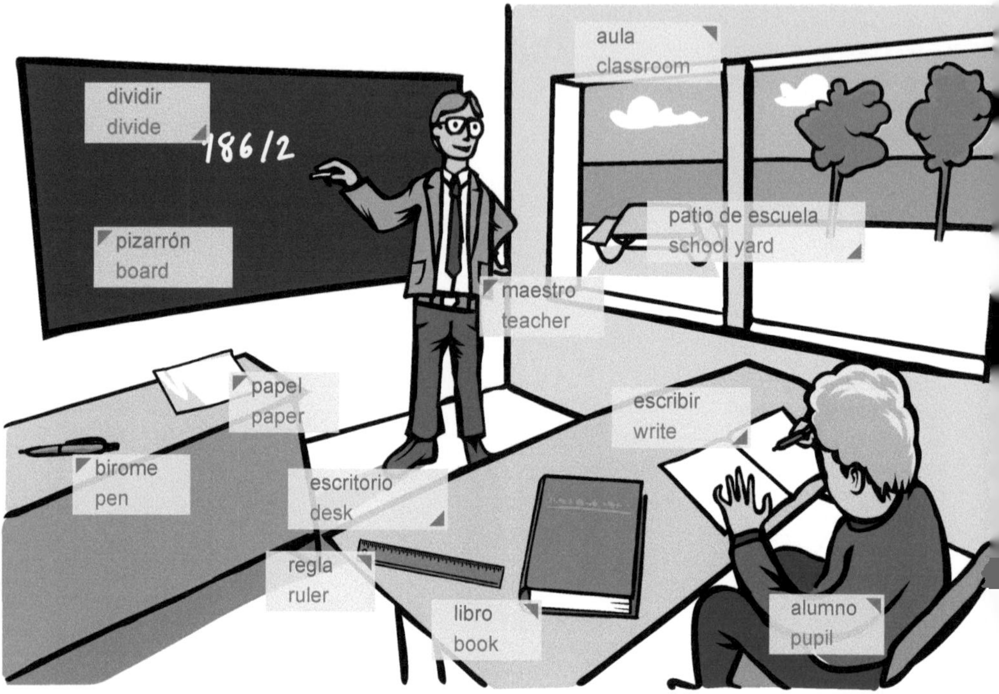
aula
classroom
dividir
divide
186/2
pizarrón
board
patio de escuela
school yard
maestro
teacher
papel
paper
escribir
write
birome
pen
escritorio
desk
regla
ruler
libro
book
alumno
pupil

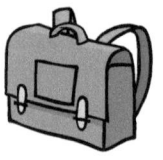

mochila

satchel

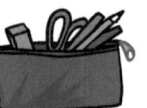

caja de lápices

pencil case

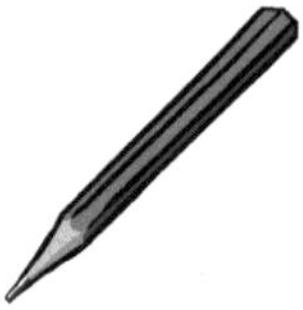

lápiz

pencil

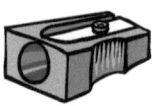

sacapuntas

pencil sharpener

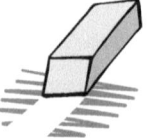

goma (de borrar)

rubber

bloc de dibujo

drawing pad

dibujo

drawing

pincel

paintbrush

caja de pinturas

paint box

tijera

scissors

pegamento

glue

cuaderno de ejercicios

exercise book

tarea

homework

número

number

sumar

add

restar

subtract

multiplicar

multiply

calcular

calculate

letra

letter

abecedario

alphabet

palabra

word

texto

text

leer

read

tiza

chalk

lección

lesson

cuaderno de clase

register

examen

exam

certificado

certificate

uniforme escolar

school uniform

educación

education

enciclopedia

encyclopedia

universidad

university

microscopio

microscope

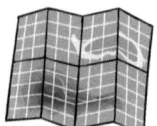

mapa

map

tacho (de basura)

paper bin

viaje

travel

hotel
hotel
Grand
hostel
hostel
ROOMS
casa de cambio
bureau de change
EXCHANGE
valija
suitcase
auto
car

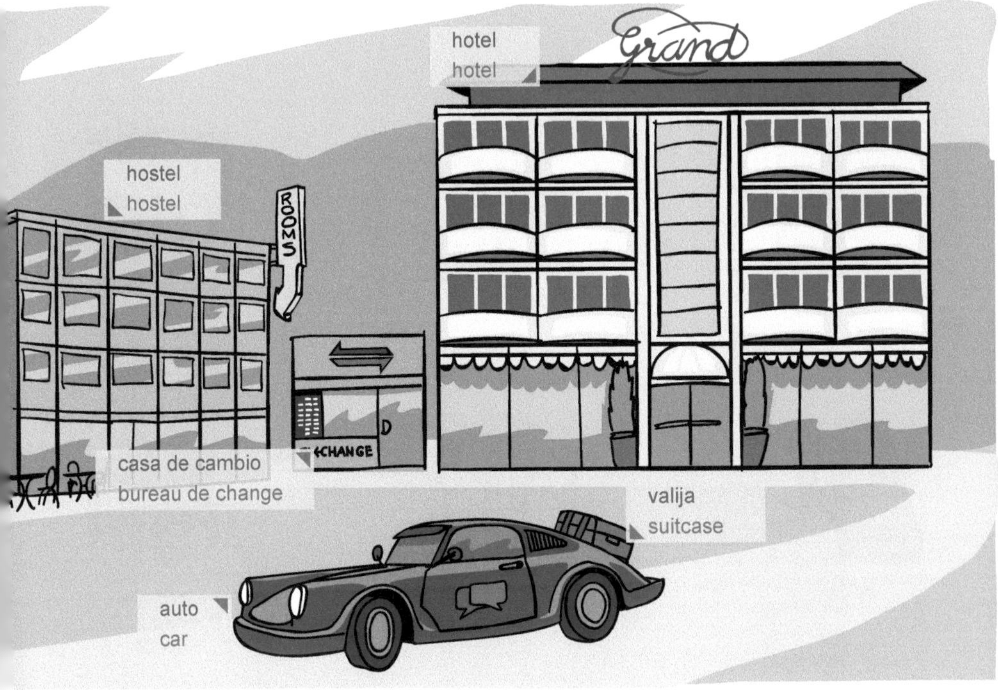

idioma

language

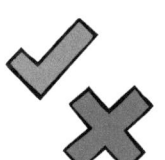

sí / no

yes / no

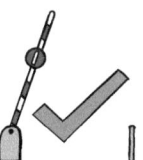

Está bien

Okay

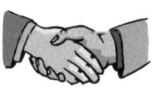

hola

hello

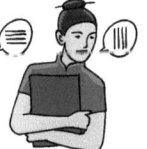

traductor

translator

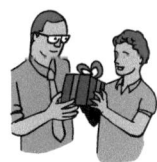

Gracias

Thank you

¿cuánto cuesta…?

how much does … cost?

No entiendo

I do not understand

problema

problem

¡Buenas tardes!

Good evening!

¡Buenos días!

Good morning!

¡Buenas noches!

Good night!

adiós

bye bye

dirección

direction

equipaje

luggage

bolso

bag

mochila

backpack

invitado

guest

habitación

room

bolsa de dormir

sleeping bag

carpa

tent

información turística

tourist information

playa

beach

tarjeta de crédito

credit card

desayuno

breakfast

almuerzo

lunch

cena

dinner

pasaje

ticket

ascensor

lift

sello

stamp

frontera

border

aduana

customs

embajada

embassy

visa

visa

pasaporte

passport

transporte
transport

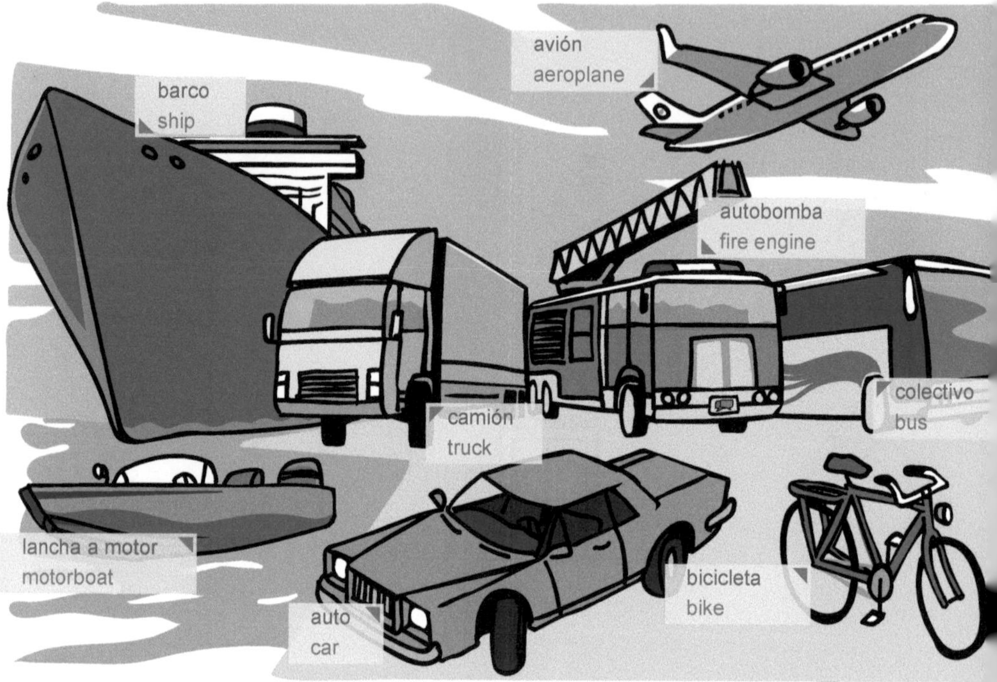
avión
aeroplane
barco
ship
autobomba
fire engine
colectivo
bus
camión
truck
lancha a motor
motorboat
bicicleta
bike
auto
car

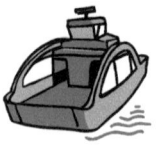

ferry

ferry

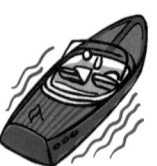

bote

boat

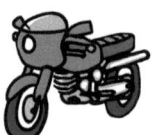

moto

motorbike

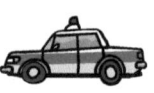

patrullero

police car

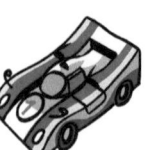

auto de carreras

racing car

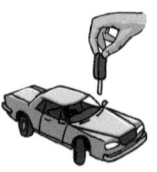

auto de alquiler

rental car

alquiler de autos

car sharing

grúa

breakdown truck

camión de basura

refuse truck

motor

motor

nafta

fuel

estación de servicio

petrol station

señal de tránsito

traffic sign

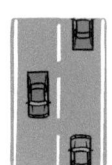

tránsito

traffic

embotellamiento

traffic jam

estacionamiento

car park

estación de tren

train station

vías

tracks

tren

train

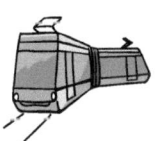

tranvía

tram

vagón

carriage

helicóptero

helicopter

aeropuerto

airport

torre

tower

pasajero

passenger

contenedor

container

caja de cartón

carton

carretilla

cart

canasta

basket

despegar / aterrizar

take off / land

ciudad

city

pueblo

village

centro de ciudad

city centre

casa

house

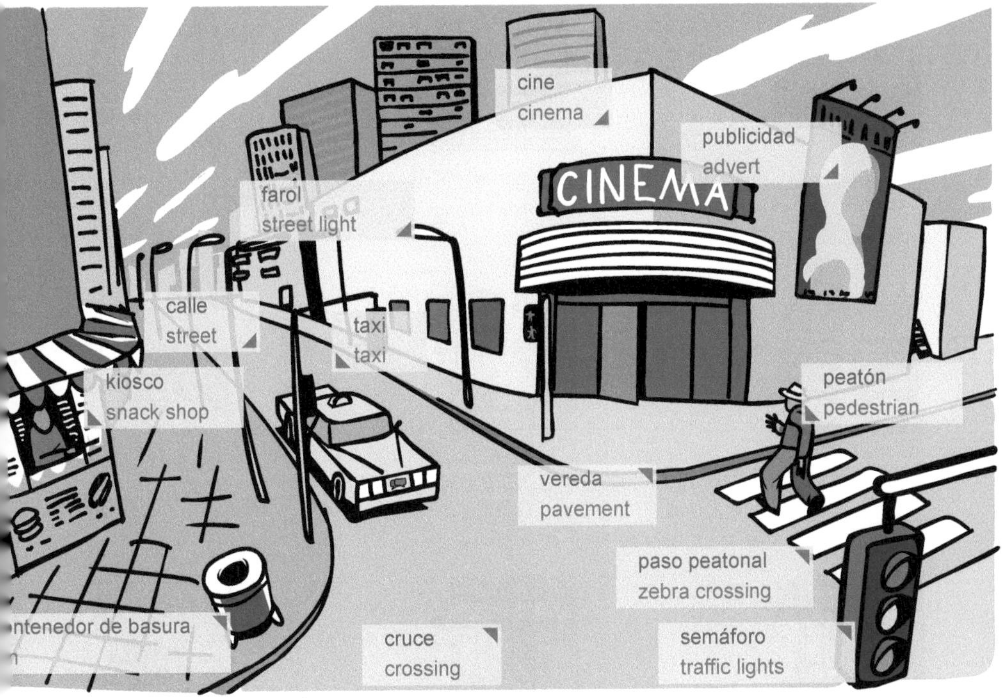

cine
cinema

publicidad
advert

farol
street light

CINEMA

calle
street

taxi
taxi

kiosco
snack shop

peatón
pedestrian

vereda
pavement

paso peatonal
zebra crossing

ntenedor de basura

cruce
crossing

semáforo
traffic lights

cabaña

hut

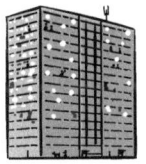

departamento

flat

estación de tren

train station

municipalidad

town hall

museo

museum

colegio

school

universidad
university

banco
bank

hospital
hospital

hotel
hotel

farmacia
pharmacy

oficina
office

librería
book shop

negocio
shop

florería
florist's

supermercado
supermarket

mercado
market

grandes tiendas
department store

pescadería
fishmonger's

centro comercial
shopping centre

puerto
harbour

parque	banco	puente
park	bench	bridge

escaleras	subte	túnel
stairs	underground	tunnel

parada del colectivo	bar	restaurante
bus stop	bar	restaurant

buzón	letrero	parquímetro
postbox	road sign	parking meter

zoológico	pileta	mezquita
zoo	swimming pool	mosque

granja

farm

contaminación

pollution

cementerio

graveyard

iglesia

church

juegos infantiles

playground

templo

temple

paisaje
landscape

hoja
leaf

poste indicador
signpost

camino
way

pradera
meadow

piedra
stone

árbol
tree

excursionista
hiker

río
river

hierba
grass

flor
flower

valle
valley

montaña
hill

lago
lake

bosque
forest

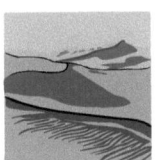

desierto
desert

volcán
volcano

castillo
castle

arco iris
rainbow

champiñón
mushroom

palmera
palm tree

mosquito
mosquito

mosca
fly

hormiga
ant

abeja
bee

araña
spider

escarabajo

beetle

rana

frog

ardilla

squirrel

erizo

hedgehog

liebre

hare

lechuza

owl

pájaro

bird

cisne

swan

jabalí

boar

ciervo

deer

alce

moose

presa

dam

aerogenerador

wind turbine

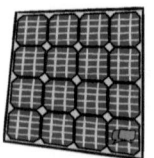

panel solar

solar panel

clima

climate

restaurante

restaurant

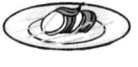

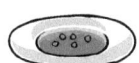

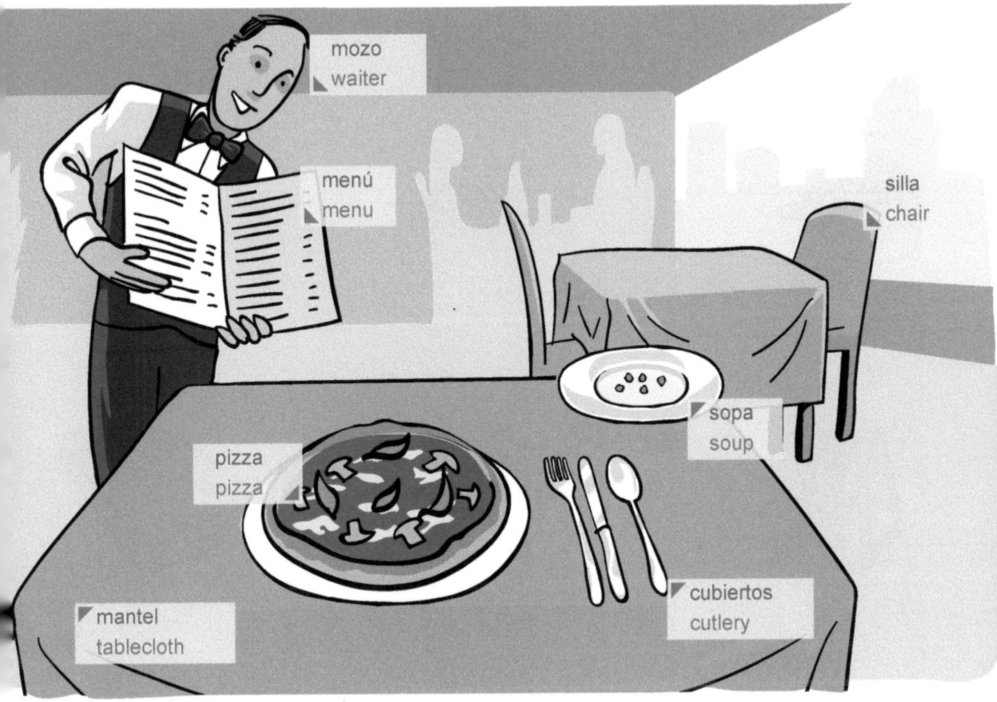
mozo
waiter
menú
menu
silla
chair
sopa
soup
pizza
pizza
cubiertos
cutlery
mantel
tablecloth

entrada
starter

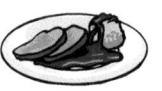

plato principal
main course

postre
dessert

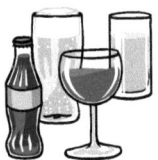

bebidas
drinks

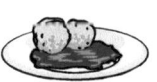

comida
food

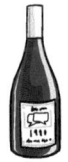

botella
bottle

comida rápida

fast food

comida callejera

street food

tetera

teapot

azucarera

sugar bowl

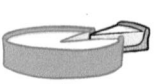

porción

portion

cafetera expreso

espresso machine

sillita alta

high chair

cuenta

bill

bandeja

tray

cuchillo

knife

tenedor

fork

cuchara

spoon

cucharita

teaspoon

servilleta

serviette

vaso

glass

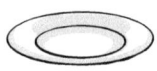

plato

plate

plato hondo

soup plate

plato

saucer

salsa

sauce

salero

salt cellar

molinillo de pimienta

pepper mill

vinagre

vinegar

aceite

oil

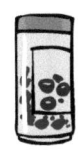

especias

spices

kétchup

ketchup

mostaza

mustard

mayonesa

mayonnaise

supermercado
supermarket

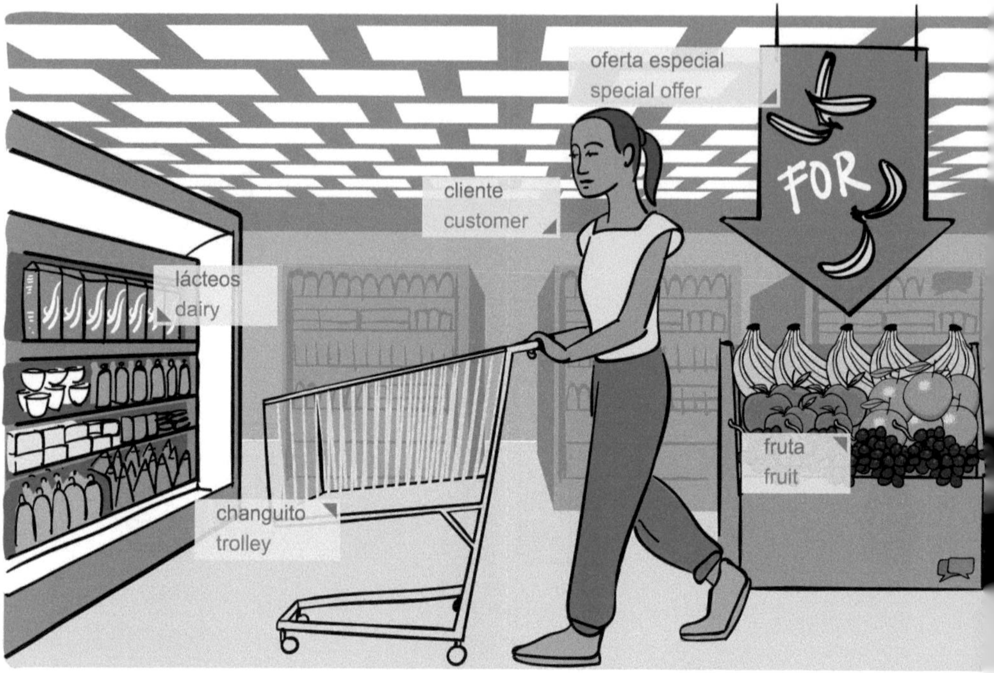

oferta especial
special offer
FOR
cliente
customer
lácteos
dairy
fruta
fruit
changuito
trolley

BUTCHERS

carnicería

butcher´s

BAKERY

panadería

baker´s

pesar

weigh

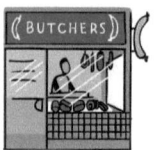

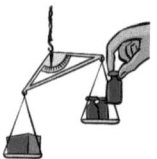

verduras

vegetables

carne

meat

alimentos congelados

frozen food

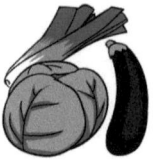

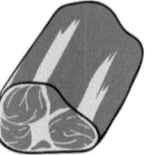

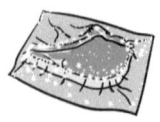

fiambres

cold meat

alimentos enlatados

tinned food

detergente en polvo

washing powder

golosinas

sweets

electrodomésticos

household products

productos de limpieza

cleaning products

vendedora

salesperson

caja

till

cajero

cashier

lista de compras

shopping list

horario de atención

opening hours

billetera

wallet

tarjeta de crédito

credit card

cartera

bag

bolsa de plástico

plastic bag

agua

water

jugo

juice

leche

milk

bebida cola

coke

vino

wine

cerveza

beer

alcohol

alcohol

cacao

cocoa

té

tea

café

coffee

café expreso

espresso

cappuccino

cappuccino

banana

banana

manzana

apple

naranja

orange

melón

melon

limón

lemon

zanahoria

carrot

ajo

garlic

bambú

bamboo

cebolla

onion

champiñón

mushroom

nueces

nuts

fideos

noodles

tallarines

spaghetti

arroz

rice

ensalada

salad

papas fritas

chips

papas fritas

fried potatoes

pizza

pizza

hamburguesa

hamburger

sándwich

sandwich

churrasco

cutlet

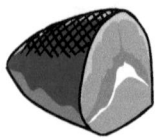

jamón

ham

salame

salami

salchicha

sausage

pollo

chicken

asado

roast

pescado

fish

copos de avena

porridge oats

muesli

muesli

copos de maíz

cornflakes

harina

flour

medialuna

croissant

pancito

bread roll

pan

bread

tostada

toast

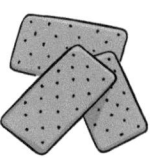

galletitas

biscuits

manteca

butter

cuajada

curd

torta

cake

huevo

egg

huevo frito

fried egg

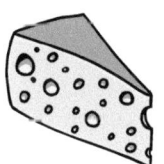

queso

cheese

comida - food

helado

ice cream

azúcar

sugar

miel

honey

mermelada

jam

pasta de chocolate

chocolate spread

curry

curry

granja
farm

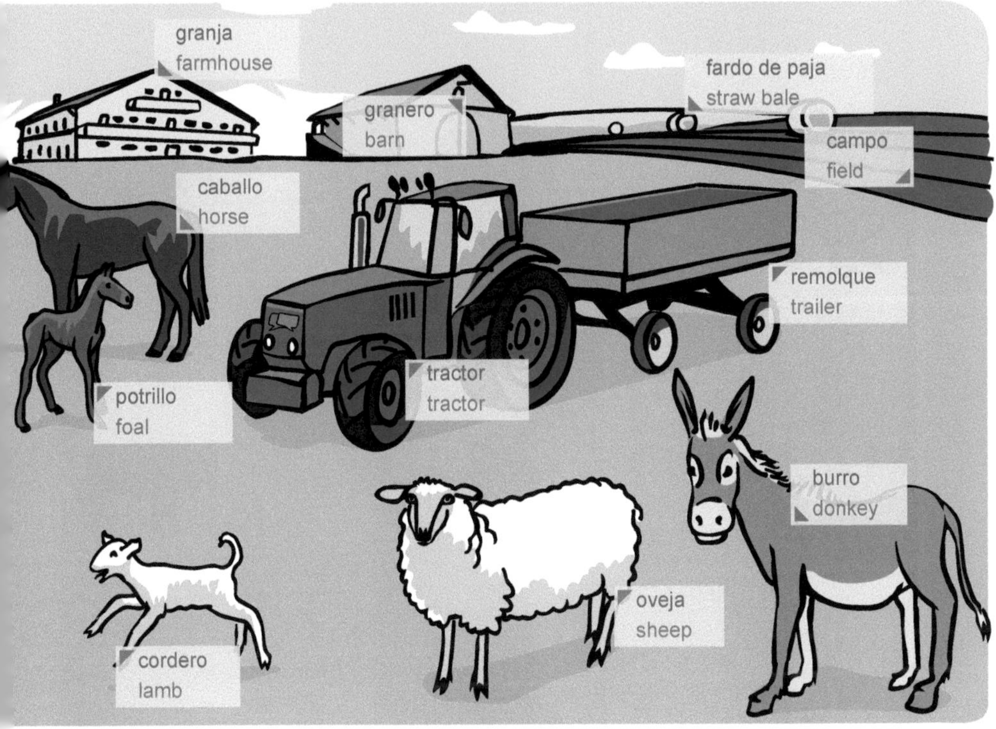
granja
farmhouse
granero
barn
fardo de paja
straw bale
campo
field
caballo
horse
remolque
trailer
tractor
tractor
potrillo
foal
burro
donkey
oveja
sheep
cordero
lamb

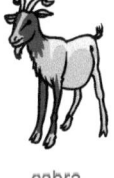

cabra

goat

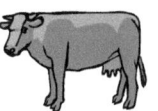

vaca

cow

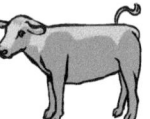

ternero

calf

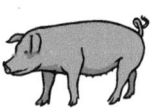

cerdo

pig

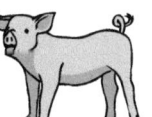

lechón

piglet

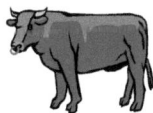

toro

bull

ganso

goose

pato

duck

pollo

chick

gallina

hen

gallo

cock

rata

rat

gato

cat

ratón

mouse

buey

ox

perro

dog

cucha

doghouse

manguera

garden hose

regadera

watering can

guadaña

scythe

arado

plough

hoz

sickle

azada

hoe

horquilla

pitchfork

hacha

axe

carretilla

wheelbarrow

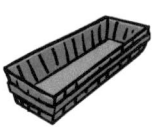

abrevadero

trough

lechera

milk can

bolsa

sack

reja

fence

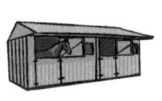

establo

stable

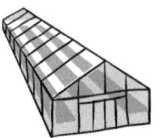

invernadero

greenhouse

suelo

soil

semilla

seed

fertilizador

fertilizer

cosechadora

combine harvester

cosechar

harvest

cosecha

harvest

batatas

yams

trigo

wheat

soja

soy

papa

potato

maíz

corn

semilla de colza

rapeseed

árbol frutal

fruit tree

mandioca

cassava

cereales

cereals

casa
house

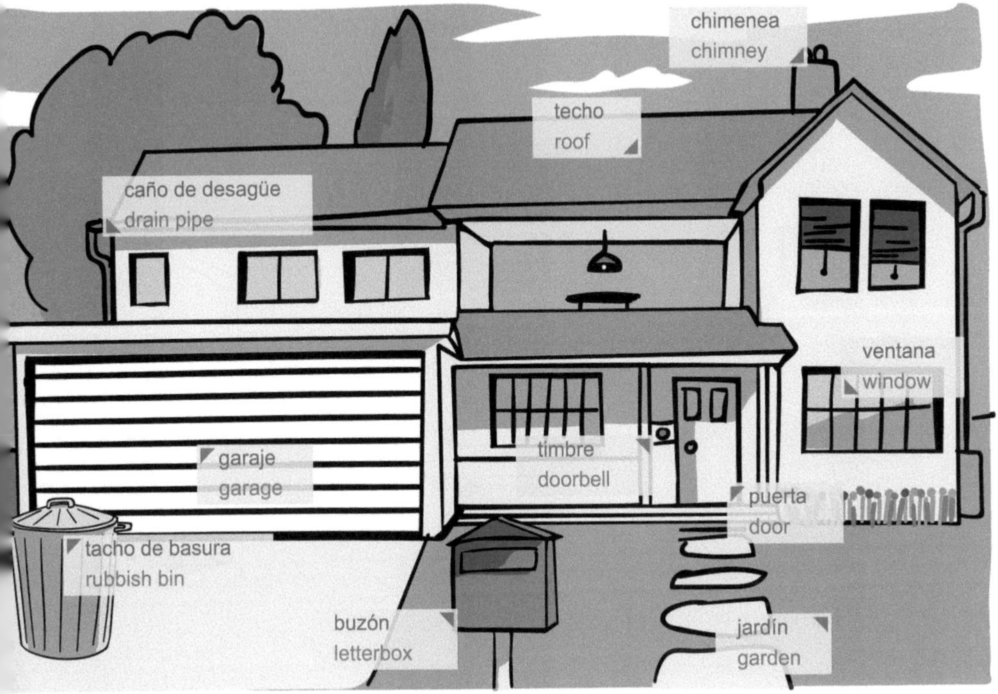

chimenea
chimney
techo
roof
caño de desagüe
drain pipe
ventana
window
garaje
garage
timbre
doorbell
puerta
door
tacho de basura
rubbish bin
buzón
letterbox
jardín
garden

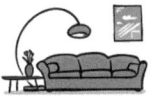

living
living room

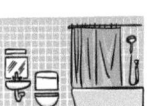

baño
bathroom

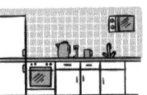

cocina
kitchen

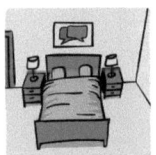

dormitorio
bedroom

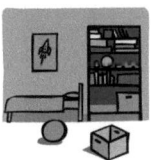

cuarto de los chicos
child's room

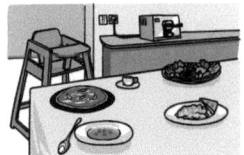

comedor
dining room

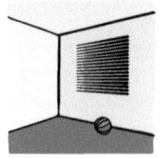

piso
....
floor

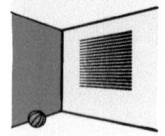

pared
....
wall

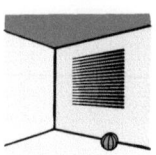

cielorraso
....
ceiling

sótano
....
cellar

sauna
....
sauna

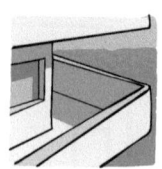

balcón
....
balcony

terraza
....
terrace

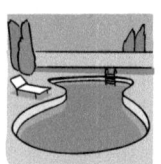

pileta
....
pool

cortadora de pasto
....
lawn mower

sábana
....
sheet

acolchado
....
bedspread

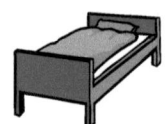

cama
....
bed

escoba
....
broom

balde
....
bucket

interruptor
....
switch

living

living room

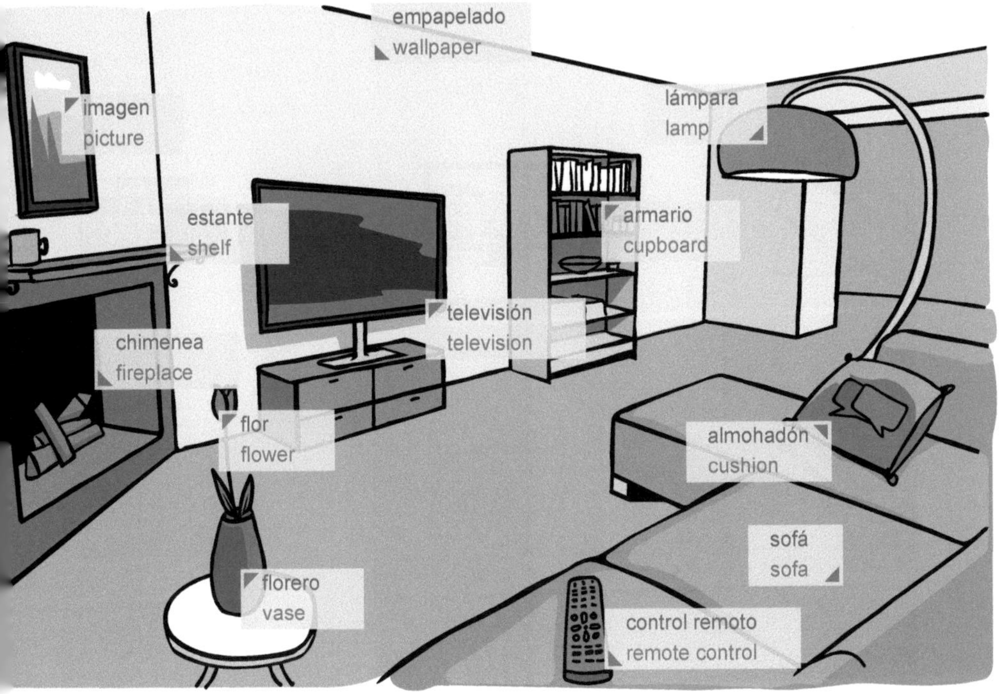

empapelado
wallpaper
imagen
picture
lámpara
lamp
estante
shelf
armario
cupboard
televisión
television
chimenea
fireplace
flor
flower
almohadón
cushion
sofá
sofa
florero
vase
control remoto
remote control

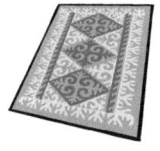

alfombra

carpet

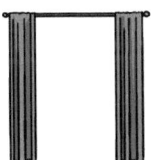

cortina

curtain

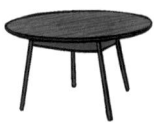

mesa

table

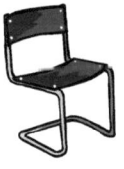

silla

chair

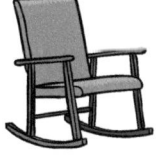

mecedora

rocking chair

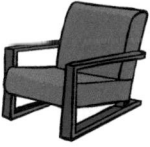

sillón

armchair

libro

book

frazada

blanket

decoración

decoration

leña

firewood

película

film

equipo de música

hi-fi equipment

llave

key

diario

newspaper

pintura

painting

póster

poster

radio

radio

cuaderno

notepad

aspiradora

hoover

cactus

cactus

vela

candle

cocina
kitchen

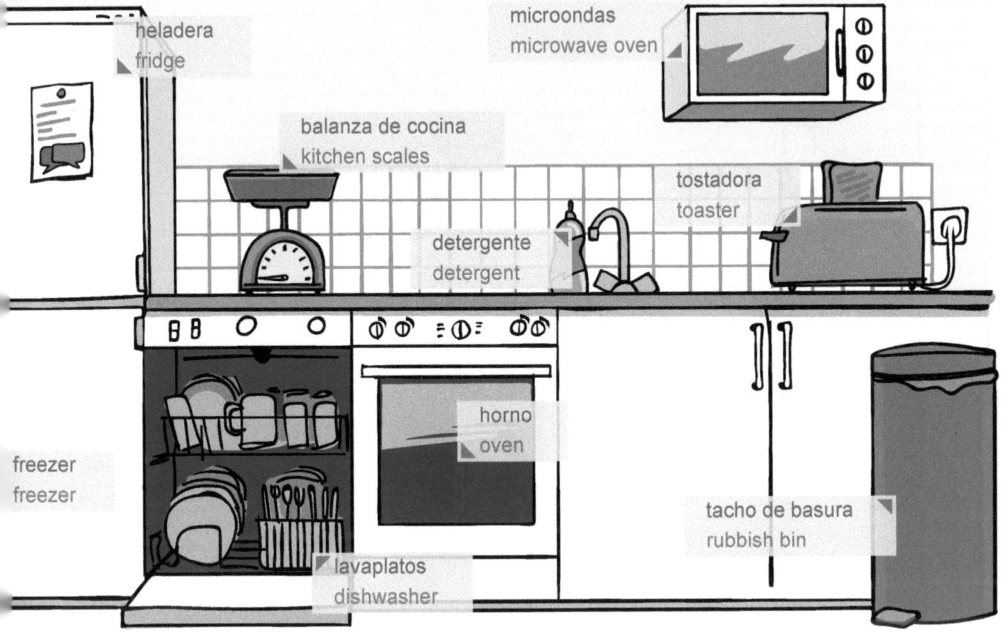
heladera
fridge
microondas
microwave oven
balanza de cocina
kitchen scales
tostadora
toaster
detergente
detergent
horno
oven
freezer
freezer
tacho de basura
rubbish bin
lavaplatos
dishwasher

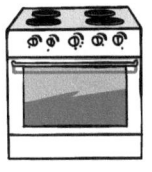

cocina

cooker

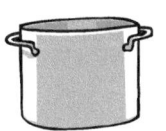

olla

pot

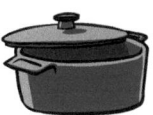

olla de hierro fundido

cast-iron pot

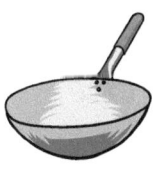

wok

wok / kadai

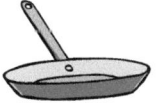

sartén

pan

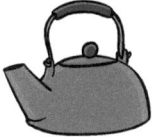

pava

kettle

vaporera

steamer

bandeja de horno

baking tray

vajilla

crockery

taza

mug

bol

bowl

palitos

chopsticks

cucharón

ladle

estpátula

spatula

batidora

whisk

colador

strainer

colador

sieve

rallador

grater

mortero

mortar

parrilla

barbecue

fogata

open fire

tabla de picar

chopping board

palo de amasar

rolling pin

sacacorchos

corkscrew

lata

can

abrelatas

can opener

manopla

pot holder

pileta

sink

cepillo

brush

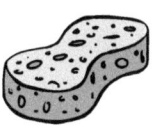

esponja

sponge

batidora

blender

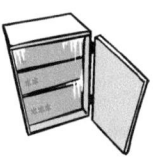

congelador

deep freezer

mamadera

baby bottle

canilla

tap

baño

bathroom

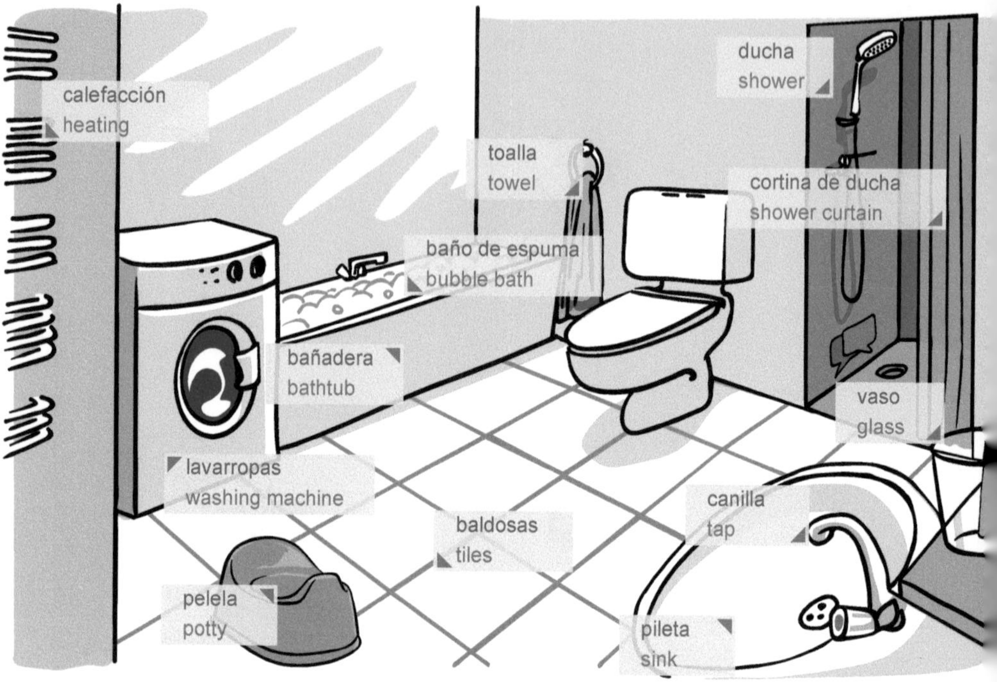

calefacción
heating
ducha
shower
toalla
towel
cortina de ducha
shower curtain
baño de espuma
bubble bath
bañadera
bathtub
vaso
glass
lavarropas
washing machine
canilla
tap
baldosas
tiles
pelela
potty
pileta
sink

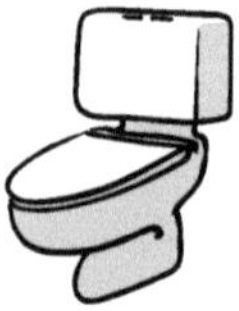

inodoro

toilet

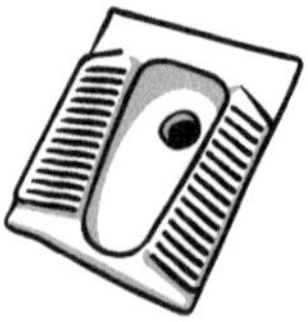

letrina

squat toilet

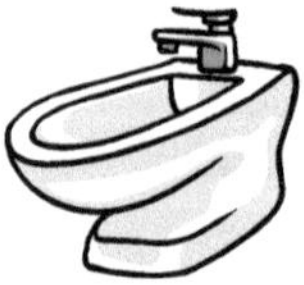

bidé

bidet

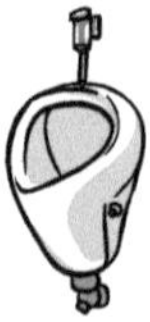

mingitorio

urinal

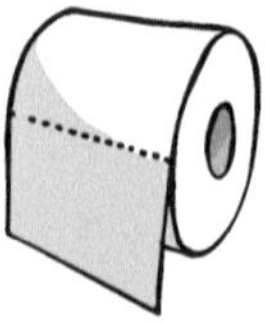

papel higiénico

toilet paper

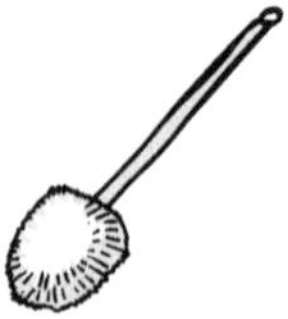

cepillo para el inodoro

toilet brush

cepillo de dientes

toothbrush

dentífrico

toothpaste

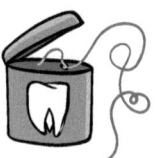

hilo dental

dental floss

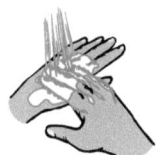
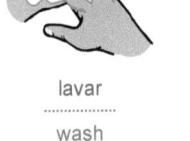

lavar

wash

ducha de mano

handheld shower

ducha higiénica

douche

palangana

basin

cepillo para espalda

back brush

jabón

soap

gel de ducha

shower gel

shampoo

shampoo

toallita

flannel

desagüe

drain

crema

cream

desodorante

deodorant

baño - bathroom

espejo

mirror

espejito

hand mirror

maquinita de afeitar

razor

espuma de afeitar

shaving foam

aftershave

aftershave

peine

comb

cepillo

brush

secador de pelo

hair dryer

spray

hairspray

maquillaje

makeup

lápiz de labios

lipstick

esmalte para uñas

nail varnish

algodón

cotton wool

tijera para uñas

nail scissors

perfume

perfume

portacosméticos

washbag

banqueta

stool

balanza

weighing scale

bata

bathrobe

guantes de goma

rubber gloves

tampón

tampon

toallita femenina

sanitary towel

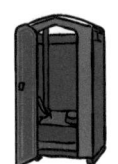

baño químico

chemical toilet

cuarto de los chicos
child's room

despertador
alarm clock
peluche
cuddly toy
coche de juguete
toy car
sonajero
rattle
casa de muñecas
doll's house
regalo
present

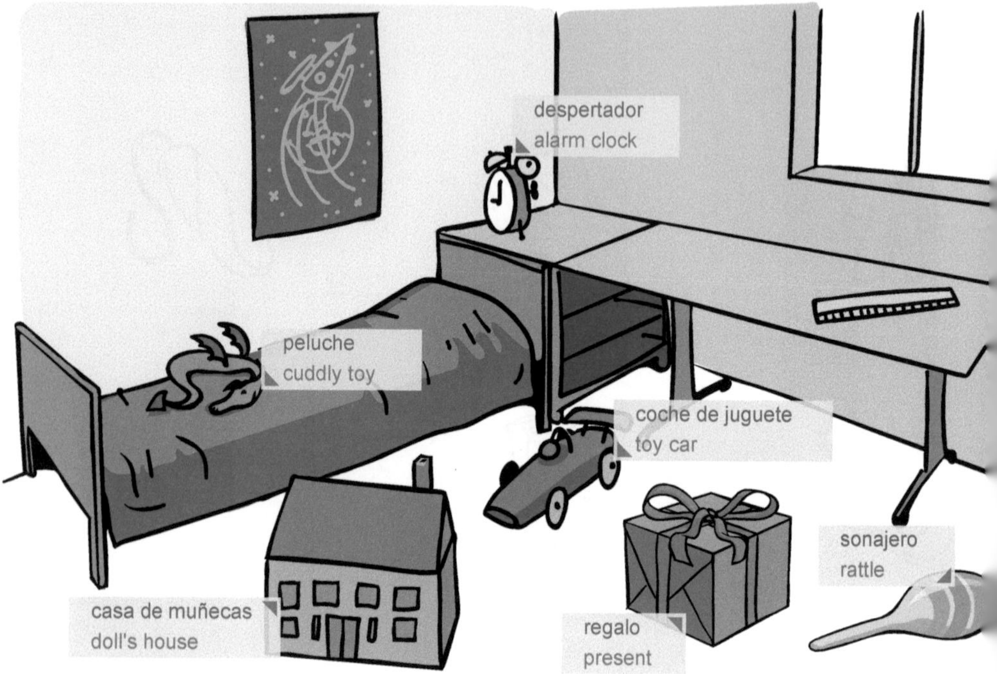

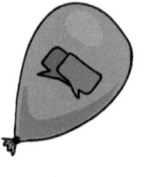

globo

balloon

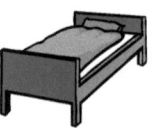

cama

bed

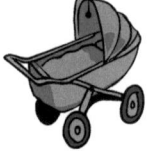

cochecito

pram

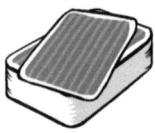

cartas

deck of cards

rompecabezas

jigsaw

SUPER
MEGA

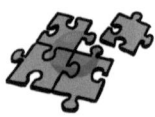

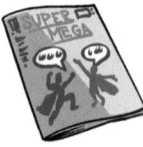

historieta

comic

piezas de lego

lego bricks

ladrillos de juguete

building blocks

figura de acción

action figure

enterito (de bebé)

romper suit

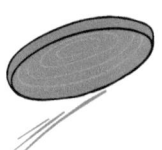

frisbee

Frisbee

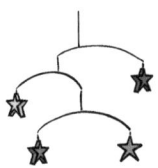

móvil para bebés

mobile

juego de mesa

board game

dados

dice

tren eléctrico

model train set

chupete

dummy

fiesta

party

libro de cuentos ilustrado

picture book

pelota

ball

muñeca

doll

jugar

play

arenero

sandpit

hamaca

swing

juguetes

toys

consola de videojuegos

video game console

triciclo

tricycle

osito de peluche

teddy bear

armario

wardrobe

ropa

clothing

medias

socks

medias panty

stockings

calzas

tights

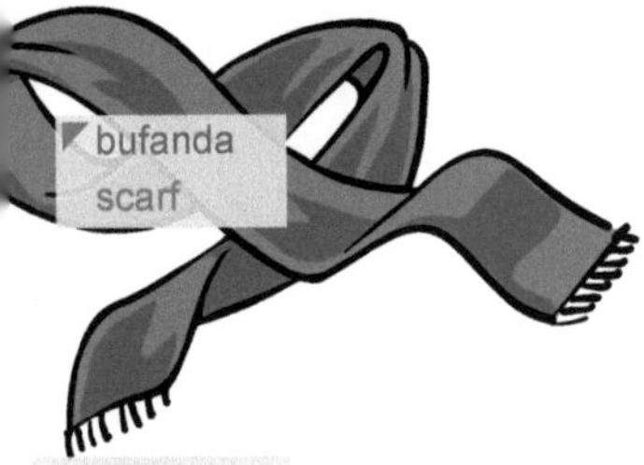

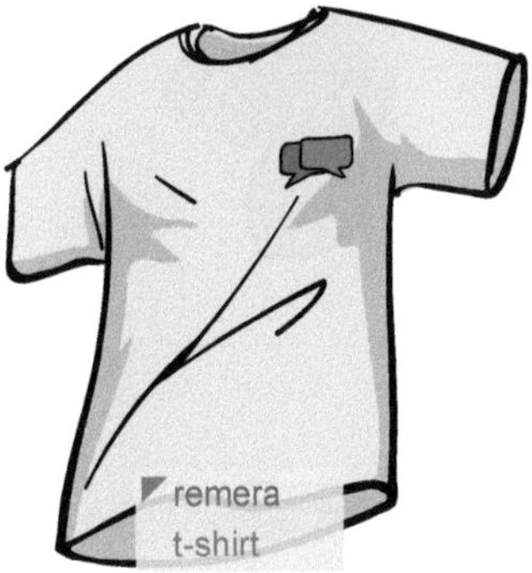

bufanda
scarf

cinturón
belt

paraguas
umbrella

remera
t-shirt

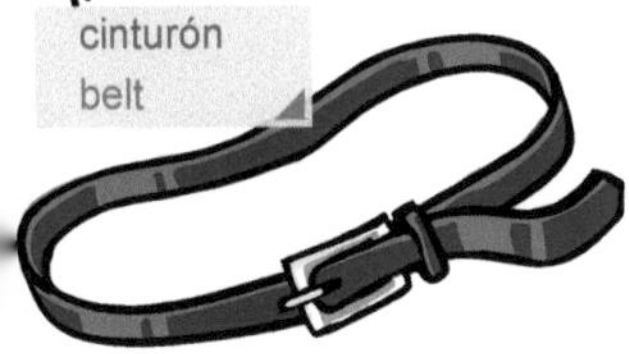

zapatillas
trainers

botas
boots

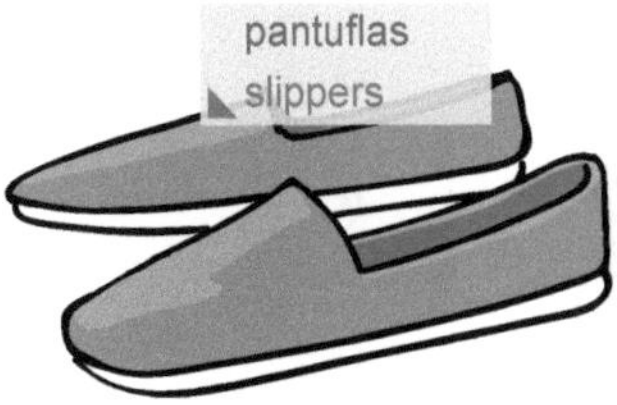

pantuflas
slippers

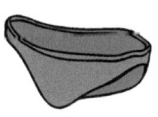

sandalias
·················
sandals

zapatos
·················
shoes

botas de goma
·················
rubber boots

ropa interior
·················
underpants

corpiño
·················
bra

chaleco
·················
vest

body
body

pantalones
trousers

jeans
jeans

pollera
skirt

blusa
blouse

camisa
shirt

pulóver
pullover

buzo
hoodie

blazer
blazer

campera
jacket

tapado
coat

piloto
raincoat

traje
costume

vestido
dress

vestido de novia
wedding dress

traje
suit

camisón
nightgown

pijama
pyjamas

sari
sari

pañuelo para cabeza
headscarf

turbante
turban

burka
burqa

caftán
kaftan

abaya
abaya

traje de baño
swimsuit

short de baño
trunks

shorts
shorts

jogging
tracksuit

delantal
apron

guantes
gloves

botón

button

anteojos

glasses

pulsera

bracelet

collar

necklace

anillo

ring

aro

earring

gorra

cap

percha

coat hanger

sombrero

hat

corbata

tie

cierre

zipper

casco

helmet

tiradores

braces

uniforme escolar

school uniform

uniforme

uniform

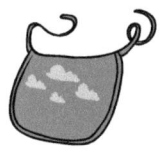

babero

bib

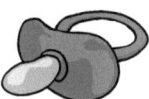

chupete

dummy

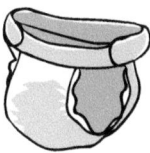

pañal

nappy

oficina
office

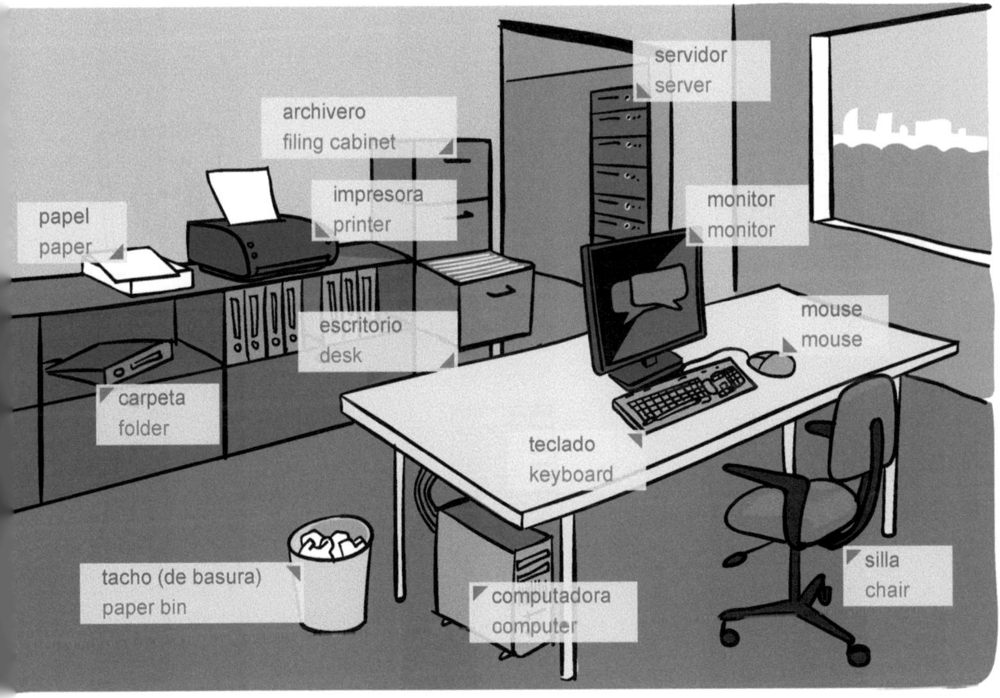
servidor
server
archivero
filing cabinet
impresora
printer
papel
paper
monitor
monitor
mouse
mouse
escritorio
desk
carpeta
folder
teclado
keyboard
tacho (de basura)
paper bin
computadora
computer
silla
chair

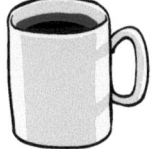

taza de café

coffee mug

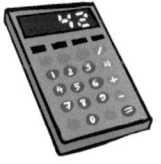

calculadora

calculator

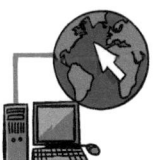

internet

internet

laptop
laptop

carta
letter

mensaje
message

celular
mobile

red
network

fotocopiadora
photocopier

software
software

teléfono
telephone

tomacorriente
plug socket

fax
fax machine

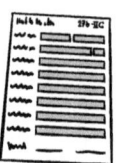

formulario
form

documento
document

comprar
buy

pagar
pay

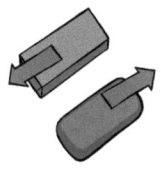

hacer negocios
trade

dinero
money

  **USD**

dólar
dollar

  **EUR**

euro
euro

  **JPY**

yen
yen

  **RUB**

rublo
rouble

  **CHF**

franco suizo
Swiss franc

  **CNY**

yuan
renminbi yuan

  **INR**

rupia
rupee

cajero automático
cashpoint

casa de cambio

bureau de change

oro

gold

plata

silver

petróleo

oil

energía

energy

precio

price

contrato

contract

impuesto

tax

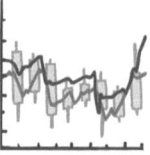

acción

stock

trabajar

work

empleado

employee

empleador

employer

fábrica

factory

negocio

shop

ocupaciones
occupations

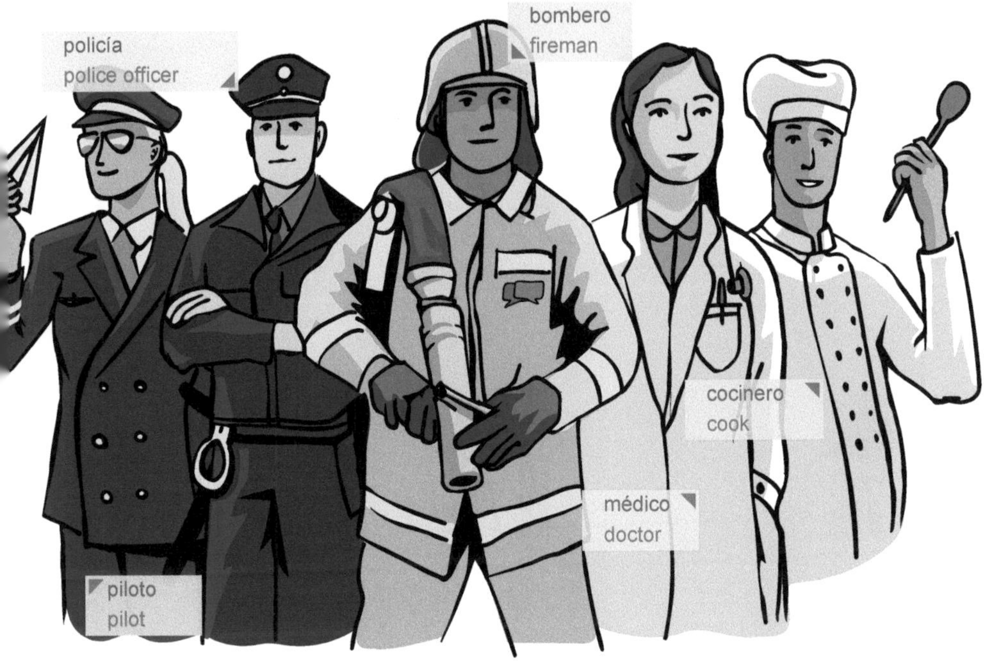
bombero
fireman
policía
police officer
cocinero
cook
médico
doctor
piloto
pilot

jardinero

gardener

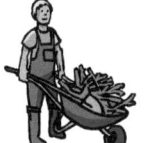

carpintero

carpenter

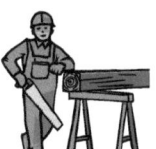

modista

seamstress

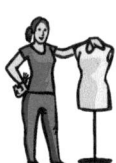

juez

judge

farmacéutico

chemist

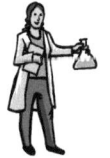

actor

actor

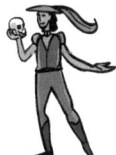

colectivero

bus driver

taxista

taxi driver

pescador

fisherman

mucama

cleaning lady

techista

roofer

mozo

waiter

cazador

hunter

pintor

painter

panadero

baker

electricista

electrician

albañil

builder

ingeniero

engineer

carnicero

butcher

plomero

plumber

cartero

postman

soldado

soldier

arquitecto

architect

cajero

cashier

florista

florist

peluquero

hairdresser

cobrador

conductor

mecánico

mechanic

capitán

captain

dentista

dentist

científico

scientist

rabino

rabbi

imán

imam

monje

monk

sacerdote

clergyman

ocupaciones - occupations

herramientas
tools

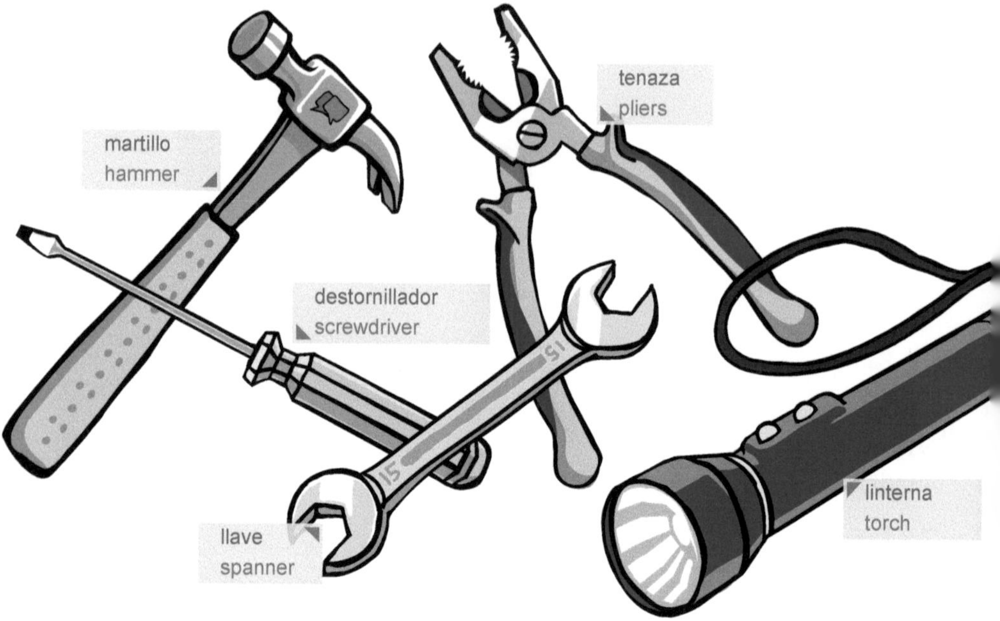
martillo
hammer
tenaza
pliers
destornillador
screwdriver
llave
spanner
linterna
torch

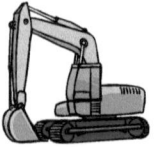

excavadora

digger

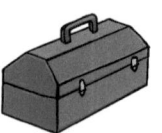

caja de herramientas

toolbox

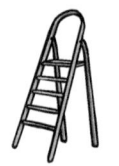

escalera portátil

ladder

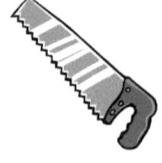

sierra

saw

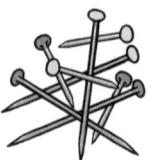

clavos

nails

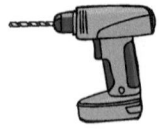

taladro

drill

arreglar

repair

pala de jardín

shovel

¡Qué bronca!

Damn!

pala de plástico

dustpan

tacho de pintura

paint pot

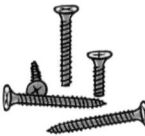

tornillos

screws

instrumentos musicales
musical instruments

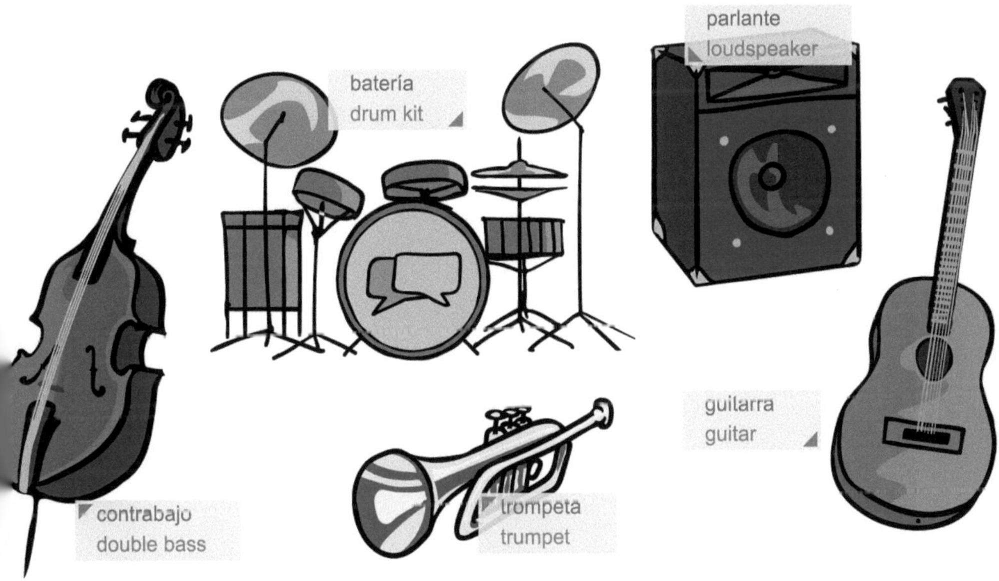

batería
drum kit

parlante
loudspeaker

guitarra
guitar

contrabajo
double bass

trompeta
trumpet

piano
piano

violín
violin

bajo
bass

timbales
timpani

tambor
drums

teclado
keyboard

saxofón
saxophone

flauta
flute

micrófono
microphone

zoológico

zoo

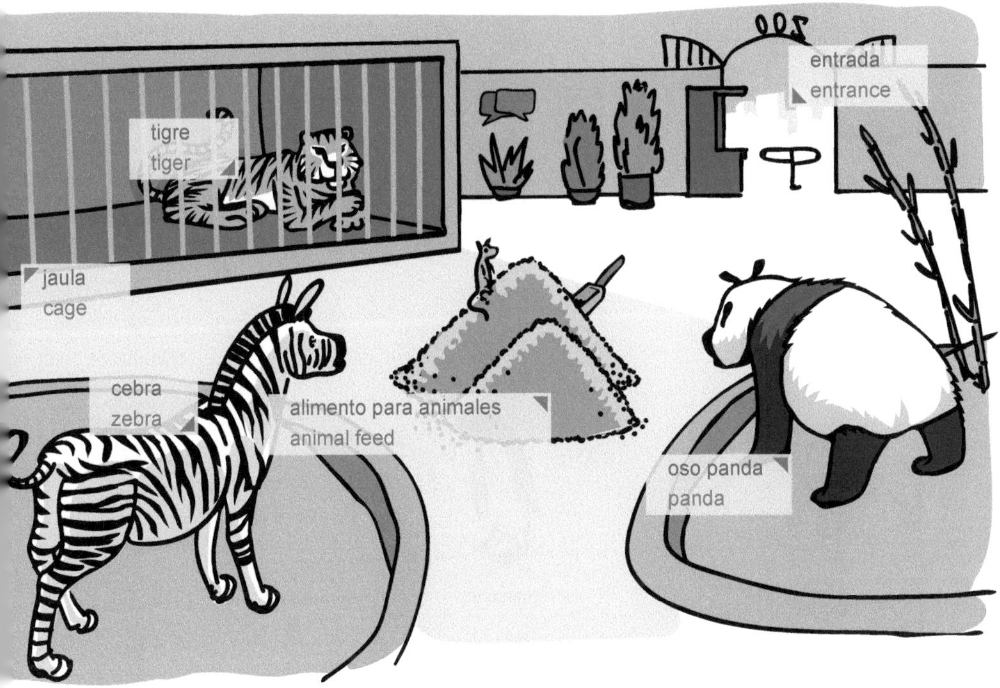
ZOO
tigre
tiger
entrada
entrance
jaula
cage
cebra
zebra
alimento para animales
animal feed
oso panda
panda

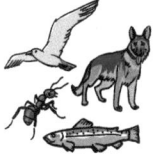

animales
animals

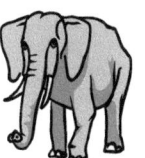

elefante
elephant

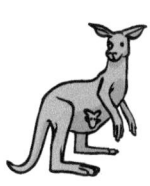

canguro
kangaroo

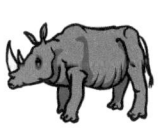

rinoceronte
rhino

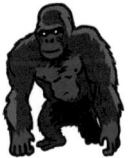

gorila
gorilla

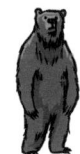

oso
bear

camello

camel

avestruz

ostrich

león

lion

mono

monkey

flamenco

flamingo

loro

parrot

oso polar

polar bear

pingüino

penguin

tiburón

shark

pavo real

peacock

serpiente

snake

cocodrilo

crocodile

cuidador del zoológico

zookeeper

foca

seal

jaguar

jaguar

zoológico - zoo

poni
pony

leopardo
leopard

hipopótamo
hippo

jirafa
giraffe

águila
eagle

jabalí
boar

pescado
fish

tortuga
turtle

morsa
walrus

zorro
fox

gacela
gazelle

fútbol americano
American football

ciclismo
cycling

tenis
tennis

básquet
basketball

natación
swimming

boxeo
boxing

hockey sobre hielo
ice hockey

fútbol
football

bádminton
badminton

atletismo
athletics

handball
handball

esquí
skiing

polo
polo

saltar
jump

abrazar
hug

reír
laugh

caminar
walk

cantar
sing

rezar
pray

besar
kiss

soñar
dream

escribir
write

dibujar
draw

mostrar
show

presionar
push

dar
give

tomar
take

tener

have

hacer

do

ser

be

estar parado

stand

correr

run

tirar

pull

tirar

throw

caer

fall

estar acostado

lie

esperar

wait

llevar

carry

estar sentado

sit

vestirse

get dressed

dormir

sleep

despertar

wake up

mirar

look at

llorar

cry

acariciar

stroke

peinar

comb

hablar

talk

entender

understand

preguntar

ask

escuchar

listen

beber

drink

comer

eat

ordenar

tidy up

amar

love

cocinar

cook

manejar

drive

volar

fly

navegar

sail

calcular

calculate

leer

read

aprender

learn

trabajar

work

casarse

marry

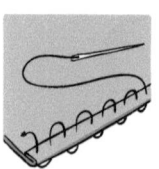

coser

sew

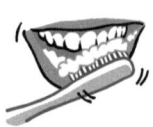

cepillarse los dientes

brush teeth

matar

kill

fumar

smoke

enviar

send

abuela
grandmother

abuelo
grandfather

padre
father

madre
mother

bebé
baby

hija
daughter

hijo
son

invitado

guest

tía

aunt

tío

uncle

hermano

brother

hermana

sister

cuerpo
body

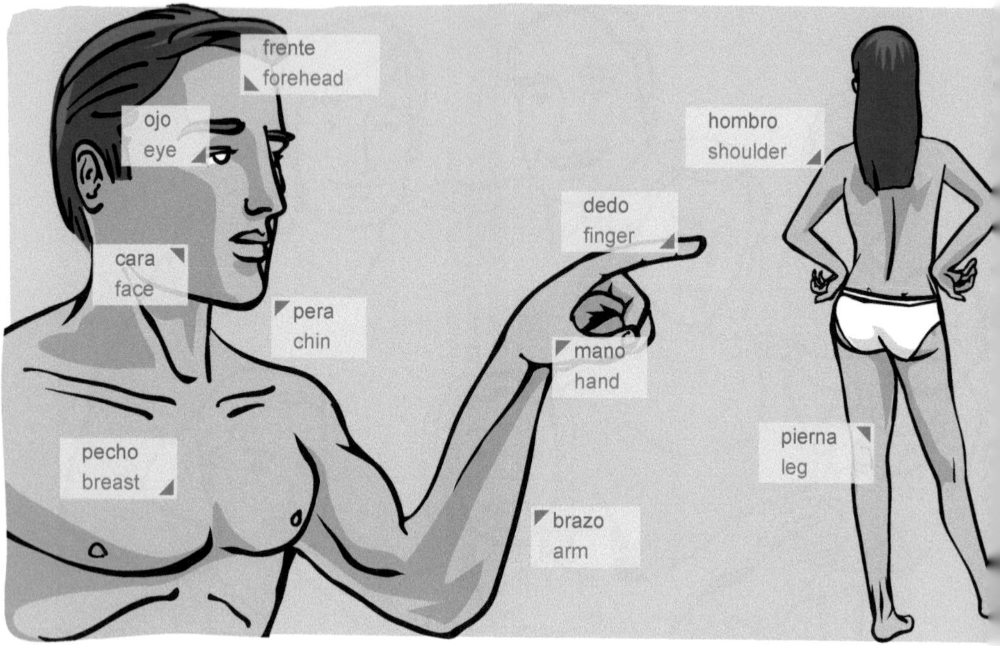

frente
forehead

ojo
eye

hombro
shoulder

dedo
finger

cara
face

pera
chin

mano
hand

pecho
breast

pierna
leg

brazo
arm

bebé

baby

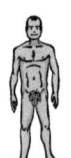

hombre

man

mujer

woman

nena

girl

nene

boy

cabeza

head

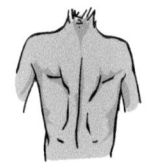

espalda

back

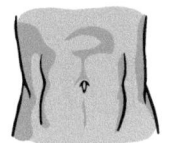

panza

belly

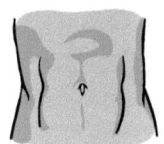

ombligo

belly button

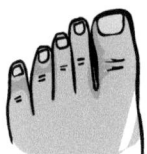

dedo del pie

toe

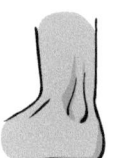

talón

heel

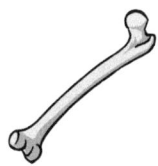

hueso

bone

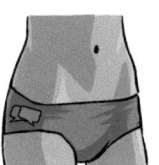

cadera

hip

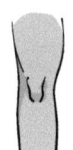

rodilla

knee

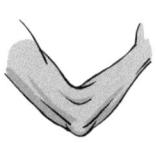

codo

elbow

nariz

nose

cola

bottom

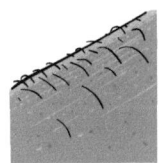

piel

skin

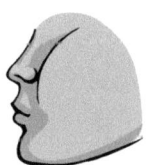

cachete

cheek

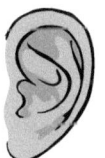

oreja

ear

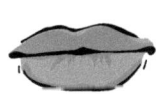

labio

lip

boca

mouth

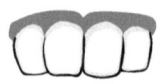

diente

tooth

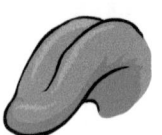

lengua

tongue

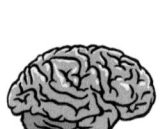

cerebro

brain

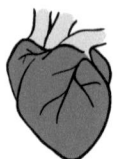

corazón

heart

músculo

muscle

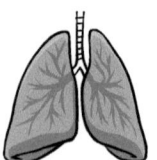

pulmón

lung

hígado

liver

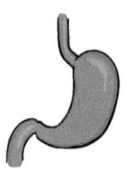

estómago

stomach

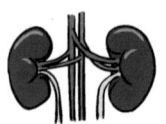

riñones

kidneys

sexo

sex

preservativo

condom

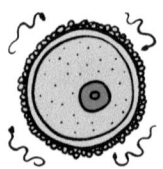

óvulo

ovum

semen

semen

embarazo

pregnancy

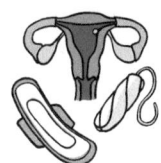

menstruación

menstruation

vagina

vagina

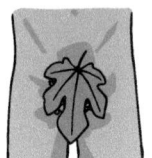

pene

penis

ceja

eyebrow

pelo

hair

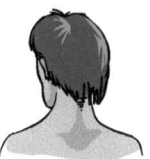

cuello

neck

hospital
hospital

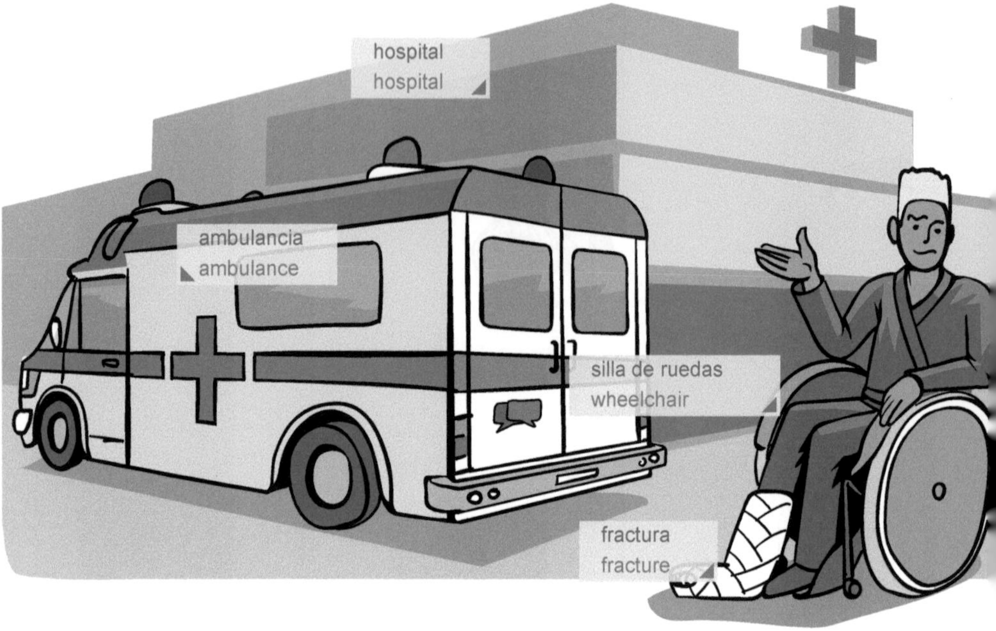

hospital
hospital
ambulancia
ambulance
silla de ruedas
wheelchair
fractura
fracture

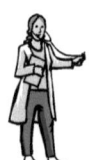

médico

doctor

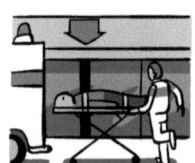

sala de guardia

emergency room

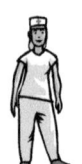

enfermera

nurse

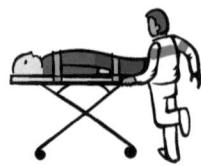

emergencia

emergency

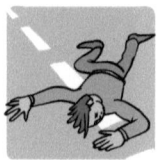

inconsciente

unconscious

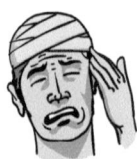

dolor

pain

lesión

injury

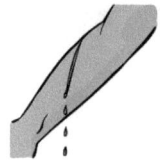

hemorragia

bleeding

infarto

heart attack

ACV

stroke

alergia

allergy

tos

cough

fiebre

fever

gripe

flu

diarrea

diarrhoea

dolor de cabeza

headache

cáncer

cancer

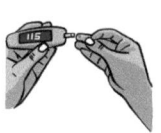

diabetes

diabetes

cirujano

surgeon

bisturí

scalpel

operación

operation

TC

CT

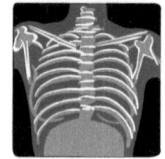

rayos x

x-ray

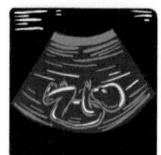

ecografía

ultrasound

barbijo

face mask

enfermedad

disease

sala de espera

waiting room

muleta

crutch

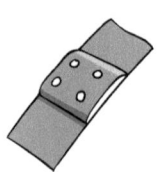

curita

plaster

venda

bandage

inyección

injection

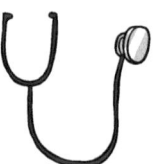

estetoscopio

stethoscope

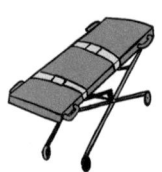

camilla

stretcher

termómetro

clinical thermometer

nacimiento

birth

sobrepeso

overweight

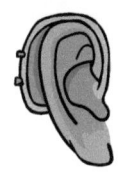

audífono

hearing aid

desinfectante

disinfectant

infección

infection

virus

virus

VIH / SIDA

HIV / AIDS

remedio

medicine

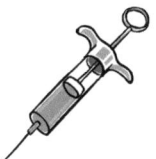

vacunación

vaccination

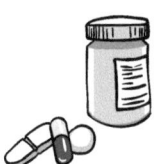

comprimidos

tablets

pastilla anticonceptiva

pill

llamada de emergencia

emergency call

tensiómetro

blood pressure monitor

enfermo / sano

sick / healthy

¡Ayuda!

Help!

alarma

alarm

agresión

assault

ataque

attack

peligro

danger

salida de emergencia

emergency exit

¡Fuego!

Fire!

matafuego

fire extinguisher

accidente

accident

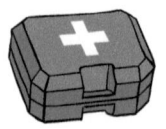

botiquín de primeros auxilios

first-aid kit

SOS

SOS

policía

police

Europa

Europe

América del Norte

North America

América del Sur

South America

África

Africa

Asia

Asia

Australia

Australia

Atlántico

Atlantic

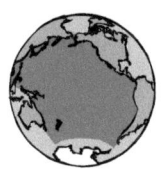

Pacífico

Pacific

Océano Índico

Indian Ocean

Océano Antártico

Antarctic Ocean

Océano Ártico

Arctic Ocean

polo norte

North Pole

polo sur

South Pole

Antártida

Antarctica

Tierra

Earth

tierra

land

mar

sea

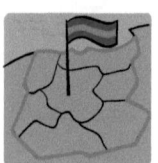

isla

island

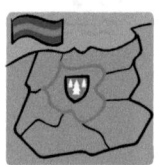

nación

nation

estado

state

esfera

clock face

manecilla de las horas

hour hand

minutero

minute hand

segundero

second hand

¿Qué hora es?

What time is it?

día

day

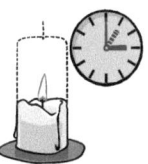

hora

time

ahora

now

reloj digital

digital watch

minuto

minute

hora

hour

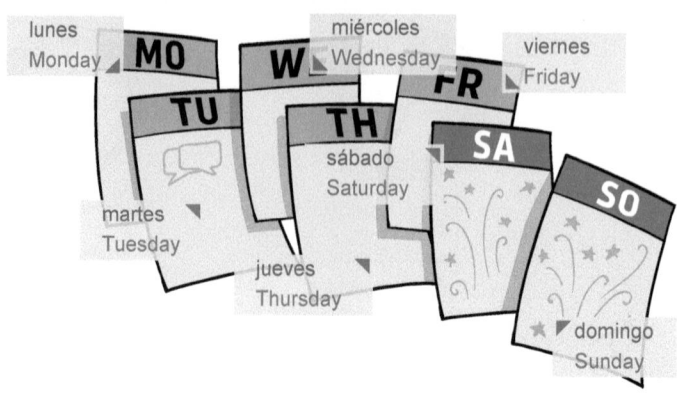

lunes / Monday
martes / Tuesday
miércoles / Wednesday
jueves / Thursday
viernes / Friday
sábado / Saturday
domingo / Sunday

ayer
yesterday

hoy
today

mañana
tomorrow

mañana
morning

mediodía
noon

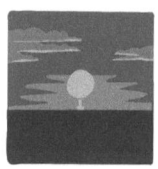

tarde
evening

MO	TU	WE	TH	FR	SA	SU
1	2	3	4	5	6	7
8	9	10	11	12	13	14
15	16	17	18	19	20	21
22	23	24	25	26	27	28
29	30	31	1	2	3	4

días hábiles
business days

MO	TU	WE	TH	FR	SA	SU
1	2	3	4	5	6	7
8	9	10	11	12	13	14
15	16	17	18	19	20	21
22	23	24	25	26	27	28
29	30	31	1	2	3	4

fin de semana
weekend

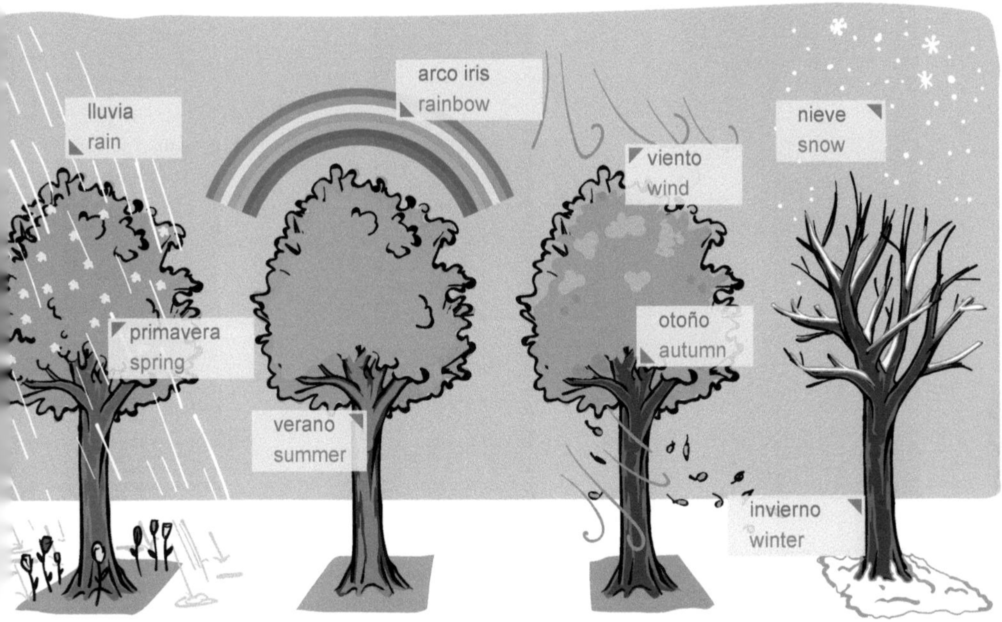

lluvia
rain
arco iris
rainbow
nieve
snow
viento
wind
primavera
spring
otoño
autumn
verano
summer
invierno
winter

4.APRIL 11°
5.APRIL 4°
6.APRIL 13°
7.APRIL 8°
8.APRIL 10°

pronóstico meteorológico

weather forecast

F C
120 40
90 30
60 20
30 10
0 0
-30 -10
-20

termómetro

thermometer

luz del sol

sunshine

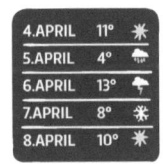

nube

cloud

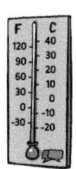

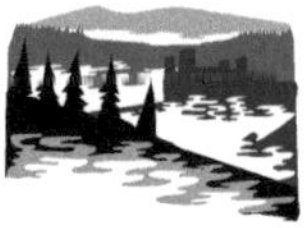

niebla

fog

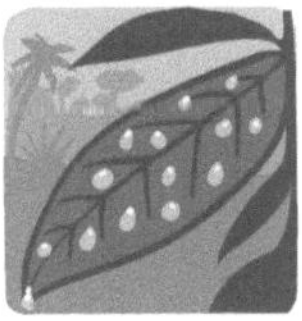

humedad

humidity

rayo

lightning

trueno

thunder

tormenta

storm

granizo

hail

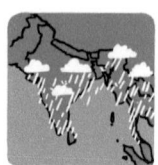

monzón

monsoon

inundación

flood

hielo

ice

enero

January

febrero

February

marzo

March

abril

April

mayo

May

junio

June

julio

July

agosto

August

82

año - year

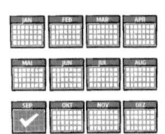

septiembre
September

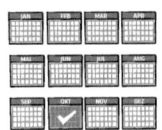

octubre
October

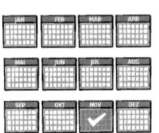

noviembre
November

diciembre
December

formas
shapes

círculo
circle

cuadrado
square

rectángulo
rectangle

triángulo
triangle

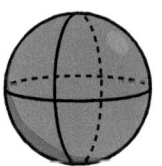

esfera
sphere

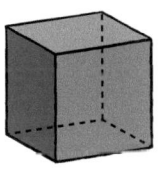

cubo
cube

blanco

white

amarillo

yellow

naranja

orange

rosa

pink

rojo

red

violeta

purple

azul

blue

verde

green

marrón

brown

gris

grey

negro

black

mucho / poco
a lot / a little

enojado / tranquilo
angry / calm

lindo / feo
beautiful / ugly

principio / fin
beginning / end

grande / chico
big / small

claro / oscuro
bright / dark

hermano / hermana
brother / sister

limpio / sucio
clean / dirty

completo / incompleto
complete / incomplete

día / noche
day / night

muerto / vivo
dead / alive

ancho / angosto
wide / narrow

comestible / no comestible

edible / inedible

malo / amable

evil / nice

entusiasmado / aburrido

excited / bored

gordo / flaco

fat / thin

primero / último

first / last

amigo / enemigo

friend / enemy

lleno / vacío

full / empty

duro / blando

hard / soft

pesado / liviano

heavy / light

hambre / sed

hunger / thirst

enfermo / sano

sick / healthy

ilegal / legal

illegal / legal

inteligente / estúpido

intelligent / stupid

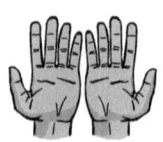

izquierda / derecha

left / right

cerca / lejos

near / far

nuevo / usado
new / used

nada / algo
nothing / something

viejo / joven
old / young

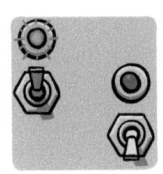

encendido / apagado
on / off

abierto / cerrado
open / closed

silencioso / ruidoso
quiet / loud

rico / pobre
rich / poor

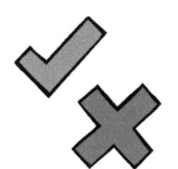

correcto / incorrecto
right / wrong

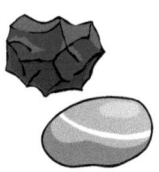

áspero / suave
rough / smooth

triste / contento
sad / happy

corto / largo
short / long

lento / rápido
slow / fast

mojado / seco
wet / dry

caliente / frío
warm / cool

guerra / paz
war / peace

opuestos - opposites

0

cero

zero

1

uno

one

2

dos

two

3

tres

three

4

cuatro

four

5

cinco

five

6

seis

six

7

siete

seven

8

ocho

eight

9

nueve

nine

10

diez

ten

11

once

eleven

12

doce

twelve

13

trece

thirteen

14

catorce

fourteen

15

quince

fifteen

16

dieciséis

sixteen

17

diecisiete

seventeen

18

dieciocho

eighteen

19

diecinueve

nineteen

20

veinte

twenty

100

cien

hundred

1.000

mil

thousand

1.000.000

millón

million

inglés

English

inglés americano

American English

chino mandarín

Mandarin Chinese

hindi

Hindi

español

Spanish

francés

French

árabe

Arabic

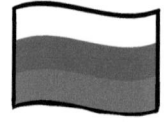

ruso

Russian

portugués

Portuguese

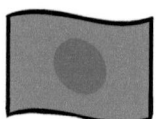

bengalí

Bengali

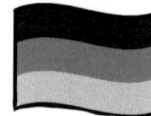

alemán

German

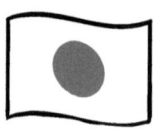

japonés

Japanese

yo

I

vos

you

él / ella

he / she / it

nosotros

we

ustedes

you

ellos

they

¿quién?

who?

¿qué?

what?

¿cómo?

how?

¿dónde?

where?

¿cuándo?

when?

nombre

name

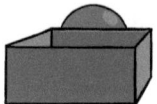

detrás

behind

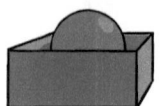

en

in

adelante de

in front of

por encima de

over

sobre

on

debajo de

under

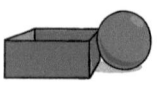

al lado de

beside

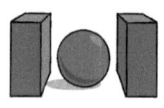

entre

between

lugar

place